Mountain's Stillness
River's Wisdom

A Compassionate Guide to the
Art of Being

Philip M. Berk

2008

"Philip's gentle poetry invites us to return to two of our primal and most faithful teachers, the spirits of water and mountain, to remember who we are and why we are here."
— Malidoma Patrice Some, Ph.D., author of *Of Water and the Spirit* and *The Healing Wisdom of Africa*

"Reading Philip M. Berk's wonderful and healing book is like breaking fresh baked bread to nourish our hungry soul."
— Hank Wesselman, Ph.D., author of *Spirit Medicine* and *Journey to the Sacred Garden*

To my beautiful daughter who continually teaches
me that miracles do come true—

And to my beautiful wife who believes in me every
step of the way—

I humbly offer this book to you as an offering from my own heart. May it uplift you and guide you into the stillness and wisdom of your own self. May it help you realize that you are perfect just as you are. May peace and blessings always be with you.

Mountain's Stillness
River's Wisdom

Table of Contents

Preface

Mountain's Stillness, River's Wisdom is a culmination of knowledge and wisdom that I have cultivated and attained through my commitment to the healing arts and my continual passion for spiritual truth. This strong passion and commitment to healing and spirituality was largely sparked by my experiences with cancer. Being faced with the reality of cancer at a very young age empowered me to live my life with a newfound strength, conviction, and purpose. In order to survive and persevere, I had to dedicate my entire life to healing. By turning my suffering into strength, my pain into inspiration, I was able to heal my life. These healing and transformative experiences have allowed me to embrace and be able to express some of the great truths of being alive—which is to be present, embrace oneself and one's life, and to continually learn to strengthen one's capacity to love.

The gift that cancer and having a life threatening disease has given me is the ability to love all of life's experiences and to be thankful to be alive. Where I used to see hardship and sorrow, I now see blessings and love. Where I used to see pain and heartache, I now see inspiration and wisdom. I have learned that once you begin to believe in yourself, anything is possible. Once you are able to transform all your fear into love, miracles will happen.

Mountain's Stillness, River's Wisdom is a book that will guide you into this magical and healing process. It is my hope that by reading these entries and reflecting upon their timeless message, you will gain a greater understanding of the wisdom that lives inside your own heart. It is my hope that this book will help you to believe in yourself and whole-heartedly trust in the power and beauty of life.

*Do not fail to learn
from the pure voice
of an ever-flowing
mountain stream
splashing over
the rocks.*
——*Morihei Ueshiba*

On Awareness

Wherever you are is
the entry point.
——Kabir

Allow yourself to feel all of life——to laugh, to cry, to work, to play, to be in pain, to be in love——to truly live. Invite everything into your life knowing that within each new experience, within each new moment you can witness and unfold the miracle of love. It is through this experience that you can embrace and accept yourself, your life, and the eternal presence of now.

The moment allows
you the freedom
to truly love

When there is love
there is no more resistance
to what is

Love brings you into the moment
with open arms,
open to whatever is

Knowing that it is
as it is
Perfect

There is no better time
than now

Now you can spontaneously
burst open in excitement

Now you can fiercely sketch
your dreams into reality

Now you can tenderly embrace
the sweetness of your life

Let go and dive in
What are you waiting for?

Your breath is the gateway
into the present moment

It guides you effortlessly
into the simplicity of what is

Within this simplicity,
you witness the clear flow of life

Within this simplicity,
you experience the gentle ease of being

All you have to do is breathe
Then each moment will gracefully unfold

Relaxing in the presence
of stillness

Accepting with the feeling
of gratitude

Opening up to the wisdom
that you are fully taken care of

This is what happens
when you enter the present moment

Now is a palace
where you sit
unmoved by the
turmoil in your life
and the futilities
in your mind

Now is a dance
that requires you
to stand up,
embrace yourself,
and cast the
rusty old shackles
away

Unlock all your closed doors!
Crumble down all your old structures!
Tear apart all your doubts and hesitations!

Forget yourself and relax
and allow the process of life
to unfold naturally within you

When you get lost in this and that
you only clog
your own natural senses

Simply, break into your heart
and reveal the ancient secret:
you are that!

All you have is the present moment—
this is where your entire life begins

Silence your need to find something else—
for there is nothing else

Forget the heaviness of the past
and experience the peace of now

Forget the mystery of the future
and experience the blessing of now

Enter this sacred reality
Open yourself to infinite possibilities

12   Philip M. Berk

On Surrender

Be grateful for whoever comes
because each has been sent
as a guide from beyond.
——*Rumi*

Life is always testing your limits and the more you willfully engage in this process, the more you inevitably feel pain—but it is what you do with the pain that matters. Just as the lotus grows out of the mud, you grow through the tests and trials that your heart endures. Your experiences, no matter how hard, are the tools for you to use to face your life. Only by surrendering to these experiences can you find the sustenance you need to keep on growing.

Surrender to what life has to offer
and you will create an opportunity
out of every situation

It is only by being humble
that you are able to make the most
out of your life

Let yourself go and know
that life will always
guide you

Let yourself go and know
that life will always
sustain you

Even though you see
how life hurts,
you still engage
in the struggle

Even though you see
how life takes,
you still embrace
all that is here

Even though you see
how hard life is,
you still give yourself
to the beauty of each new day

You cannot control the outcome
of your experience—
You can only control yourself
and the way you engage in the process

The quality of your life
depends on how you respond
to whatever life presents you

You can greet life's uncertainties
with patience and trust,
or you can greet them
with resistance and fear

The choice is completely yours

When you trust in life
you instantly stop struggling

When you trust in yourself
you instantly start believing

You instantly start seeing that deep within you
is everything you will ever need

You realize that there is nowhere to go,
but where you already are

You realize that there is nothing to do,
but simply *be* yourself

You can hold on to what was
or what could have been,
or you can let go
and feel the freedom of what is

Release the heavy burden
that your fear creates
Release the discomfort
that your insecurity brings

Once you free yourself
of all that you do not need,
you will find the courage
to accept whatever comes your way

Be gentle with yourself
and allow things to be

Be present with yourself
and allow yourself to feel

Be at ease with yourself
and allow things to flow

Return to the quiet
that is always within you

Return when your mind
has forgotten your truth

Return when your eyes
cannot see clearly

Return when you have become lost
and entangled in suffering

Return when you feel
there is nowhere left to go

24   Philip M. Berk

On Healing

Your pain is the breaking
of the shell
that encloses
your understanding.
—Kahlil Gibran

Healing is the journey. The destination is yourself. The full recognition of all the different aspects of yourself—your joy, your sorrow, your pain, your pleasure—all lead you to the source of who you are. Only by having intimate contact with this source can you experience the fullness of your life. Only by fearlessly looking within can you embrace the landscape of your life and open yourself completely to all the love and compassion that lives inside you.

Your struggle
becomes your fuel,
your sustenance,
and your power
to generate
complete awareness
in all you face

Like the art of alchemy
turn your pain
into strength,
turn your hardship
into compassion,
turn your heartache
into wisdom

It is your own responsibility
to make your life sacred
The power to transform yourself
lies within your own hands

Respect each and every emotion
that arises within you

Know that it is within each passing emotion
that life embraces you

Allow yourself to be embraced
and the process of healing naturally unfolds

Allow yourself to be healed
and the process of life naturally flourishes

Deep inside your heart
where it is tender,
where it hurts,
is exactly where you begin

Have deep reverence
for the immense beauty
that is stored there

Bow down
and lay a flower
at the altar
of your heart

It is here that
you find
the treasures
of your life

There is no better medicine
than loving yourself
There is no better cure
than allowing yourself
to be as you are

It is time to let your truth
burn inside of you
like a million suns
lighting up your way,
like a galaxy of love
surrounding your every
breath

Allow yourself to fall into the depths
knowing that you will
be reborn again

Just as spring's blossoms
renew the cold winds of winter,
you will be renewed

Know that life moves in continuous cycles
and that to every ending there is always
a new beginning

So, let yourself free-fall into the unknown
and let the restorative power within nature
be your faithful guide

Within your own pain
lies the antidote
for you to heal

Within your own heart
lies the mystery
for you to unravel

Within your own time
lies the journey
for you to embark

By embracing
what is difficult,
you witness
the healing power
of compassion

By being intimate
with your experience,
you unfold
the healing power
of love

By living
with an open heart,
you remain fearless
to the many lessons
life has to teach you

36   Philip M. Berk

On Becoming

I feel it now; there's a power in me
to grasp and give shape to my world.
I know that nothing has ever been real
without my beholding it.
All becoming has needed me.
My looking ripens things
and they come towards me
to meet and be met.
——Rainer Maria Rilke

Whatever calls you on your path, whatever signs you see, whatever dreams weave their mysteries around you—you must take heed. The process of becoming has to do with the process of accessing your own personal power and using it in a way that furthers your growth. By believing in yourself and in the process of life, you realize that you have the power to manifest your highest truth.

Fearlessly give birth
to the new you

The one that is always
reinventing herself

The one that is always open
to learning new things

The one that continually drinks
from life's healing waters

Ask yourself,
"What is it that I truly want in my life?"
Then ask yourself,
"How can I actualize all that I want in my life?"

Once you realize that the only barriers
to freeing yourself are your own barriers,
you can start believing in yourself
and in all that you are capable of

You can shine light and nourish
the seeds of all your aspirations
You can spark the tremendous potential
of all that you have ever wished for

You are the architect
of your own happiness

You create your own thoughts
through the power of your will

You create your own focus
through the power of your intention

You create your own conviction
through the power of your word

By creating and living your own happiness,
nothing can stand in your way

Mountain's Stillness, River's Wisdom   43

Fill yourself to the brim
with the things you most love to do
and you will overflow
with great passion

Fill yourself to the brim
with your inner truth
and you will overflow
with tremendous personal power

Fill yourself to the brim
with endless wonder and curiosity
and you will overflow
with an enormous exuberance for being alive

Further yourself and face
all that frightens you

You will turn
all your obstacles into allies

You will strengthen
your capacity to connect to all things

Connecting and persevering—
this is the foundation of true practice

You have the choice and freedom
to make the most out of your time

What you invest your energy in
is what you become

Like a potter that molds her pots,
you mold your life

Listen to your own inner calling
You will know exactly what to do

Create your life
into a masterpiece

Like musicians
that weave songs

Like poets
that speak to stars

Like painters
that touch visions

Dream…
the entire world is yours

On Inspiration

To see the world in a grain of sand,
and to see heaven in a wild flower,
hold infinity in the palm of your hands,
and eternity in an hour.
——William Blake

Inspiration allows a complete openness to life. This openness will bless and sustain you with its healing and restorative power. This miraculous intimacy allows you to behold the essence of your being, express the truth of your soul, be in awe of the world, see into the nature of your experience, and let go into the mystery of life.

You are free to soar
into the land of Spirit

The land where you know
without knowing

The land where you discover
without searching

The land where you are perfect
through imperfections

By continually visiting this holy land,
you will always be inspired

Be an artist
Be aware
of all that you see

Be an artist
Perceive things
with a sense of wonder

Be an artist
Be immersed
in the wellspring of creation

Be an artist
Illuminate the light
out from the darkness

Look closely
into the nature of your experience
You will find that in every situation
there lies a hidden treasure
waiting for you

Even within the simple tasks
of your everyday reality,
there lie many wondrous gifts
filled with all the inspiration
you will ever need

Through the ordinary
you discover
the extraordinary
By seeing the unseen
you enlighten all your days

Your senses are the medium
by which you experience life

By skillfully honing your senses
you enter sacred space

Within this sacred space
you become completely open

Within this sacred space
you become fully receptive

Attune yourself to this open channel
and life will always reveal itself to you

With your body open and relaxed,
you experience the truth of this new moment

With your heart open and pure,
you receive the many blessings of Spirit

With your mind open and awake,
you perceive the true nature of reality

With your soul open and connected,
you awaken and inspire your greatest presence

Feel the vibrancy of nature
Let it astound and overwhelm you

Like a colorful mandala
drawing you inwards

Like the stillness of a mountain
standing untouched by time

Like the crimson sunset
penetrating the evening landscape

Appreciating beauty in all that you see,
you will always know the source

Spirit is the key
that opens your eyes
to life

It is the key that unlocks
your intuition
and cleanses your perceptions

It is the key that fuels
your spontaneity
and inspires your art

It is the key that unleashes
your creativity
and energizes your entire being

60   Philip M. Berk

On Celebration

What is this precious love
and laughter
budding in our hearts?
It is the glorious sound
of a soul
waking up.
——Hafiz

Feel the freedom that comes when you are at peace with yourself. Feel the blessings that come when you open your heart to everyone and everything. Feel the ease of being playful, the excitement of being alive, the joy of embracing your life. When you give yourself away to love, you get the whole world back in return. When you give yourself away to love, every day becomes a wondrous celebration.

Be daring
Release your fear—
Receive endless blessings
from the Divine

Be daring
Forget your worry—
Become completely
absorbed in stillness

Be daring
Recite the healing mantra—
That, with love, anything—
and I mean anything, is possible

Completely let go of yourself
and receive the greatest bliss

Give up every need and attachment
and make room for the healing energy of grace

The power of grace flows through you
when you sacrifice your needs for a greater need

Why not experience the absolute bliss
and ecstasy of pure being?

Why not experience the absolute paradise
and heaven of living in love?

Celebrate life
and witness it magically unfold

Celebrate time
and open up the reservoirs of joy

Celebrate love
and shine light on all things

Celebrate yourself
and behold life's greatest blessing

Love unconditionally,
everything that was once difficult
will become easy

Love unconditionally,
everything that was once complicated
will become simple

Love unconditionally,
everything that was once broken
will become whole

When you return to joy,
you return to yourself

When you return to love,
you return to the source

When you return to your soul,
you return home

You are the holy seed of creation!
You are the beating heart of the universe!
Wake to your luminous nature
and feel this powerful spirit within

You are sparked with a passion for life
and every day is a living testimony
to the abundance of joy and bliss
that lives inside you

Grab hold of the miraculous
and attune yourself to the infinite

Because everything is vibration,
you harmonize yourself to divine frequencies

Because everything is love,
you resonate with all of creation

As clear and pristine as a mountain stream,
you behold the stillness and wisdom
of your true self

72   Philip M. Berk

On Realization

Approach it and there is no beginning;
follow it and there is no end.
You can't know it, but you can be it,
at ease in your own life.
Just realize where you come from;
this is the essence of wisdom.
—Lao Tzu

By letting go of the need to control, you let in the quiet witness that is the messenger of peace. See through these eternal eyes. See the true nature of Self, unbound by the many distinctions that stifle its infinite and endless nature. No thoughts can ever know it. Energy is the flow of space and time merging with the wild and raw nature of existence. Feel this flow and know that you can harness and ride it. You can breathe it in each and every moment. All the power in the cosmos is nowhere but within you. Your task is to wield its enormous power and generate its healing effects.

Let the river's wisdom
drench you

Let the continual stream
of change rush through you

Be as fluid and graceful as a dancer
moving with the current

Lose yourself in this flow,
and things will unfold with ease

You will feel the presence of peace
within everything that you do

When you love yourself,
you love all things

When you lose yourself,
you become all things

When you believe in yourself,
you have faith in all things

Trust yourself completely
Merge gracefully into all that is

It's not about doing, it's about being

Be still and quiet within—
you will find your true presence

Live within this presence—
you will not worry about expectations;
you will not concern yourself with outcomes

Firm in yourself and in your own conviction,
you will always be at peace

The nature of reality
is like a mirror that perfectly reflects
the interconnectedness of all things

Look into this mirror
See yourself whole and unified,
free from inner conflict

Look into this mirror
See the whole world as one,
free from separation

Selflessly look into this pure mirror
Free your mind
and everything else around you

Gently offer all that you have
to everyone and everything

You will be like a great sun shining,
nourishing all who enter your presence

You will be like a deep reservoir
for all to drink from

When you give all of yourself,
there will never be anything lacking

When you give all of yourself,
you will heal the entire world

Contentment arises when you open your heart
to the impermanence that pervades all things

By letting things come and go,
you accord with the natural flow of things

You see how you are in all things,
and all things are in you

Inwardly you know that there is nothing to
    achieve—
that you are the path and the goal

Awakening to wisdom,
you discover that you are the source

Within yourself—within your sacred heart
all of creation whispers

Deep inside you hear
a silent, unfathomable echo

Deep inside you feel
a mystical, enlightening breath

Connecting to this ancient source,
you will always know the way

84   Philip M. Berk

Quotations that were used in *Mountain's Stillness, River's Wisdom: A Compassionate Guide to the Art of Being* were taken from the following books:

Tao Te Ching. Translated by Stephen Mitchell. New York: HarperCollins Publishers, 1988

Art of Peace. Translated by John Stevens. Boston: Shambhala Publications, 1992

The Gift. Translated by Daniel Ladinsky. New York: Penguin Books, 1999

Rilke's Book of Hours: Love Poems to God. Translated by Anita Barrows and Joanna Macy. New York: Riverhead Books, 1996

Rumi: The Book of Love: Poems of Ecstasy and Longing. Translated by Coleman Barks. New York: HarperCollins Publishers, 2003

The Portable Blake. Edited by Alfred Kazin. New York: Penguin Books, 1976

A Touch of Grace: Songs of Kabir. Translated by Linda Hess and Shukdev Singh. Boston: Shambhala, 1994

Gibran, Kahlil. *The Prophet*. New York: Alfred A. Knopf, Inc., 1966

You can order more copies of *Mountain's Stillness, River's Wisdom: A Compassionate Guide to the Art of Being* at your local bookstore or you can order it at the following websites:

1) *Amazon.com*

2) *Borders.com*

3) *Alibris.com*

4) *Abebooks.com*

If you would like to contact the author, you can e-mail him at <u>riverswisdom@gmail.com</u> and for further information about him, please visit his website at philipmberk.com.

Made in the USA
Monee, IL
30 November 2022

19069390R00072